A PEOPLE OF DESTINY

FINDING YOUR PLACE IN GOD'S APOSTOLIC ORDER

BARBARA WENTROBLE

Wagner Publications

A People of Destiny
Copyright © 2000
by Barbara Wentroble
ISBN 1-58502-005-2

Published by
Wagner Publications
11005 N. Highway 83, Suite 119
Colorado Springs, CO 80921

Rights for publishing this book in other languages are contracted by Gospel Literature International (GLINT). GLINT also provides technical help for the adaptation, translation, and publishing of Bible study resources and books in scores of languages worldwide. For further information, contact GLINT, P.O. Box 4060, Ontario, CA 91761-1003, USA, Email: glintint@aol.com, or the publisher.

1 2 3 4 5 6 7 8 9   06 05 04 03 02 01 00

This book is dedicated to Jim and Jean Hodges.
Your revelation of apostolic ministry has sparked a passion in me to reach my destiny. Your mentoring and friendship over the years has been priceless beyond words. Your lives have significantly influenced thousands.

TABLE OF CONTENTS

◆

CHAPTER ONE

THE CHURCH IS CHANGING!

My husband's parents had just moved from Pennsylvania to Texas. I was happy to help them move into their new home. Getting the refrigerator arranged was a job I thought could be easily handled. After a couple hours of wiping out the refrigerator and filling it with food, I stood back to take a final look at my accomplishment. Everything looked neat and in order. In fact, I was proud of my work.

Then shortly thereafter, I noticed my father-in-law standing in front of the refrigerator. He was pulling everything out. What was wrong? "The mayonnaise is in the wrong place. I always put the milk on the left side and not the right side. Pickles belong on the third shelf rather than the second shelf," he commented.

After watching him spend the next half-hour rearranging the refrigerator, I realized what the problem was. I had brought change. My father-in-law was a creature of habit. He liked to have the food in the same spot it had been in for the past 30 years. My way of arranging the refrigerator had not been bad, but it was different from his traditional way.

A Modern-Day Reformation

What a picture of the Church today! The Lord is speaking change to the Church. However, it is sometimes difficult for us to embrace change. After all, the Church has been doing things the same way for many years. Why should we change? How can we benefit from this change? What will it cost us? How do we know that it is God bringing about this change? Is there any historical precedent for this change? What will the changed Church look like?

These are legitimate questions. The Lord does not expect us to embrace every new thing that comes along. In fact, He encourages us to be like the Berean believers and check out new doctrines and practices with Scripture (see Acts 17:10-11), which we must and will do. Many church leaders do agree, however, that the Church is in the midst of a major shift; the Church is in a modern-day reformation.

Webster defines the word *reform* as: "to make better by removing faults and defects, to correct; to make better by putting a stop to abuses or malpractices or by introducing better procedures."[1] Most people agree that the Church needs a reformation that will help us reach the lost more effectively. The Body of Christ also needs greater levels of training and activation for ministry. Each minister should be able to fulfill the call of God without the pressure of fitting into a mold that is contrary to his or her giftings. What kind of modern-day reformation could bring such changes to the Church?

The Restoration of Apostles

Apostles are a major part of the reformation taking place in the Church. In fact, the resurgence of apostles in the Church today is actually a restoration of God's original plan. In the early church apostles were key to the spreading of the gospel. The word *apostle* in the Greek language is *apostolos*.[2] The primary meaning is "to send." There are more than 80 occurrences of the Greek form of this word in the New Testament. Apostles are those who are sent with a message. They are ambassadors commissioned to transmit the message of the one who sent them.

The non-Greek meaning of apostles gives a nautical picture. The picture is of a fleet of ships sent to a distant place. An admiral leading the fleet would be like an apostle. In the Old Testament kings, governors, or rulers were types of apostles. Many prophets functioned in the dual ministry of apostle and prophet.

The Lord Jesus established the Early Church with all the ascension-gift ministries fully functioning. Ephesians lists them along with their purpose in chapter four, verses 11-13. Paul wrote that when Jesus left the earth and went to be with the Father, He gave gifts to His Church. These gifts are in the form of people. They are apostles, prophets, evangelists, pastors, and teachers. It is amazing that the Church today is very familiar with the gift of pastor, in spite of the fact that the word is only used one time in the New Testament. However, the Church is not as familiar with the gift of apostle even though the word and its derivatives are used more than 80 times in the New Testament.

Paul said that these five key gifts—including apostles—would be operative in the Body of Christ until we come into unity and become a mature Church in the fullness of the stature of Jesus (Eph. 4:13). The ascension-gift ministries are given to equip believers, so they, in turn, can fulfill their ministries. Since that has not happened, apostles must still be on the earth. Why then have they not been recognized in most churches? Let's pursue that question.

Great Beginnings

Apostles have not been recognized in most modern-day churches because the Church drifted away from the model of the Early Church. Somewhere along the way the Church lost the diversity of spiritual gifts that were functioning in the book of Acts. The loss, however, was not God's plan for His Church.

The Church was birthed on the day of Pentecost and grew vigorously. In those days the use of the ascension ministry gifts listed in Ephesians 4:11 were the rule rather than the exception. Supernatural signs, wonders, and miracles occurred frequently. The sick were healed, lepers were cleansed, and the dead were raised. Deliverance from evil spirits was considered the norm. Lives were radically changed as people received the power of the cleansing blood of Jesus. Church members operated in the fruits of the Holy Spirit. There was fellowship and the sharing of earthly goods for the benefit of the Body of Christ. The Church expected the Lord Jesus to do through them what He had done while He walked the earth.

The Church of that day believed it was possible to do the last thing Jesus spoke to them before He departed to heaven, which was to fulfill the Great Commission (see Matt. 28:18-20). History records Christians preaching throughout the world. The gospel was preached by the first generation of believers to every known continent and people group. Within two short years, all of Asia and the known world of that day had heard the gospel. Jews as well as Gentiles had heard the message of Jesus (Acts 19:10; Col. 1:23).

The Church's Dark Days

Sadly, the Church did not continue in the same spirit and power of the early church. Many factors contributed to the deterioration. Most church historians believe the Edict of Toleration caused the most damage. Constantine released this decree after he had a vision in October, 312 AD. Christianity then became the state religion. Up until that time, Christians were often persecuted *for their faith*. After the release of the edict, people were persecuted *for not being Christian*.

After 312 AD members of the Church included a great number of unbelievers who merely joined an institution to escape persecution. The Church moved away from the supernatural power of God into a system of dead works, formalism, and legalistic religion. Many people who came out of pagan

---

When one generation fails to be obedient to the Lord, He waits for another generation to rise up. He looks for a people who will seek to follow Him and be light in a world of darkness.

---

religions and joined the Christian church brought their rituals and religious customs with them. Emphasis which had been on an inner spiritual life and a personal relationship with Jesus shifted to obedience to rituals, pagan customs, and the religious dogmas of their leaders. Corruption, immorality, and bloodshed among the clergy were frequent. Fewer and fewer church members walked in the true worship and purity of heart that the Lord requires. Instead, members did whatever it took to survive. The Church became apostate, replacing former loyalty to Christ with empty religion. As a result, light went out in the Church.

There is a spiritual principle which teaches us that whatever happens in Church affects the world. God put His power and Spirit into the Church to change the world. Therefore, when light went out in the Church, light went out in the world. The world then entered a period of history known as the Dark Ages, which lasted from the fifth century until the fifteenth century. God's original intent for the Church became gravely obscured.

The Protestant Reformation

When one generation fails to be obedient to the Lord, He waits for another generation to rise up. He looks for a people who will seek to follow Him and be light in a world of darkness. During the fifteenth century God found such a man in a young monk by the name of Martin Luther. Luther became an instrument of the Lord to usher in a generation of believers who were part of the new Protestant Reformation. Rather than a religion of works, he preached, *"The just shall live by faith"* (Rom. 1:17).

As a result of his salvation experience with the Lord Jesus, Luther began receiving revelation from the Word of God. He saw the difference between where the Church of his day was and where the Church of the book of Acts had been. Truths taught by Luther were not new to God; they were only new to Luther and his generation. When light came into the Church, light came into the world. The world started coming out of the Dark Ages and entered a period of time known as the Industrial Revolution. What happens in the Church affects the world!

The New Apostolic Reformation God's New Order

The Lord has continued to restore truth to His Church since the days of Martin Luther. He has promised a Church without spot, wrinkle, or blemish (Eph. 5:27). This Church will be used by the Lord to cause the knowledge of the glory of the Lord to fill the earth (Hab. 2:14). The Lord today is bringing the Church into another phase of restoration. Dr. C. Peter Wagner calls the restoration now taking place "The New Apostolic Reformation." He says it is the greatest change since the days of the Protestant Reformation. That is a profound statement which leads us to believe that the Church of the twenty-first century will not look like the Church of the twentieth century.

I call the change we are now in the midst of "The New Order." The Greek word for order is *taxis*. The Zodhiates lexicon defines order *(taxis)* as: "an arrangement or discipline; to place in one's proper place."[3] The Lord is setting His house in order. He is putting the living stones in their proper place (1 Pet. 2:5). Whatever we call this new time of restoration, we know we are going to need grace for the radical change in the ways of the Church.

Intended From the Beginning

God's plan for His Church has never changed. As we see in Genesis 1, God gave a mandate to humanity in the Garden:

"Then God said, 'Let Us make man in Our image, according to Our likeness; and let them rule over the fish of the sea and over the birds of the sky and over the cattle and over all the earth, and over every creeping thing that creeps on the earth.' God created man in His own image, in the image of God He created him; male and female He created them. God blessed them; and God said to them, 'Be fruitful and multiply, and fill the earth, and subdue it; and rule over the fish of the sea and over the birds of the sky and over every living thing that moves on the earth'" (Gen. 1:26-28).

The human race was created to be God's representative in the earth. We were to guard and care for all of God's creation under His direction. Although many generations have failed in this responsibility, God has not changed His mind. He sent Jesus to restore all that had been lost to humanity. Through His death, burial, resurrection, and ascension to the right hand of God, Jesus restored our authority in the earth. Jesus' last words before returning to heaven were a repeat of the mandate given in the Garden. *"And Jesus came up and spoke to them, saying, 'All authority has been given to Me in heaven and on earth. Go therefore and make disciples of all the nations, baptizing them in the name of the Father and the Son and the Holy Spirit . . .'"* (Matt. 28:18-19).

The New Order for the Church of Jesus Christ will help restore the ministries and supernatural power God intended from the beginning. The Church will come into the completion of God's plan as spelled out by the prophet Haggai: *"The glory of the latter house will be greater than the glory of the former"* (Hag. 2:9). Adam and Eve did not fulfill God's entire plan for their lives. The Early Church did not finish the plan of God. But, Jesus is building His Church. He promised the gates of hell would never be able to stop His plan. The Church is going through reformation and into the New Order. The restoration of the ascension-gift ministries, particularly that of the gift of apostle, will change the world as it changes the Church

Notes

[1] Michael Agnes, *Webster's New World College Dictionary*, (New York, NY: Macmillan, 1999), p.1204.

[2] Spires Zodhiates, *The Hebrew – Greek Key Study Bible*, New American Standard (Chattanooga, TN: AMG Publishers, 1984; revised edition 1990), p.1810.

[3] Ibid., p.1879.

CHAPTER TWO

———◆———

CHALLENGES IN TRANSITION

The Valuable and Necessary

The day had arrived. It was Saturday and I was at home. We would be moving into our new house in a few weeks. Before the move, we had to do what every family does before they move. We had to clean out the attic!

Early that Saturday morning my husband, Dale, and I started bringing boxes down out of the attic. Where did they all come from? How did we collect so many boxes in such a few short years? Regardless of their origin or how long they had collected dust, each box had to come down for inspection. Today would be a day of sorting through everything. Anything we could live without had to go. Only those things that were valuable or necessary would remain for the move. We just didn't know how many items fit the category of *valuable* or *necessary*.

I watched as Dale carefully went through each box. He was having trouble finding *anything* that needed to be thrown away. One box contained wire. There was fat wire, skinny wire, coated wire, uncoated wire, short wire, long wire, and almost any kind of wire imaginable. "Do you think we can throw some of this wire away?" I asked.

"Barbara," he replied, "you never know when you might need some wire!"

Dale and I continued going through the boxes. Another box contained old electrical wall outlet covers. Some were covered in paint while others were covered in dirt. "Do you think we can throw away some of these outlet covers?" I asked.

"Barbara," he again replied, "you never know when you might need some of these."

We finally began sorting through dozens of cans of screws, nuts, bolts, and nails. Many were rusty. Others were bent or damaged in some way. Once again I asked, "Do you think we can get rid of some of these cans of hardware?"

Again, he replied, "You never know when you may need a nail or something to hang a picture."

How difficult it was to convince him that we were moving into a new house and it would take many years before any of these items could be used. Later in the day, a stack of boxes was piled next to our yard for the trash man. How hard it had been for Dale to release those *valuable* treasures he had owned for so many years. However, we both realized we could not take into the new place everything we had in the old place. It would not fit. We could only take into the new place those things that would still be valuable or necessary.

A Time of Transition

As God brings change to the Church, the same principle applies. He is sorting out those practices, methods, and structures that are no longer valuable or necessary for the new season of reformation. Before the Church can fully enter the new season, there is a time of change or transition.

Webster defines the word *transition* as: "a passing from one condition, form, stage, activity, place, etc. to another; the period of such passing."[1] The Church is in a time of passing from one condition or stage to another. The book of Ecclesiastes tells us that God has such times for us: *"There is an appointed time for everything. And there is a time for every event under heaven"* (Eccl. 3:1).

During this season, the Church will experience changes in several areas. They will include evangelism, body ministry, church life, and government. Our spiritual diet will be different. New connections and leadership changes will take place. Fresh vision will be released.

The Joshua generation experienced a major change after the Moses generation. Yet, God promised He would be the same. *"No man will be able to stand before you all the days of your life. Just as I have been with Moses, I will be with you; I will not fail you or forsake you"* (Josh. 1:5). Although there will be many changes, the promise of the Lord will be the same. God will be with us and not fail us.

"That's Not the Way We've Done Things Before!"

Old methods of doing things are difficult to change. Even when the old way doesn't work, we sometimes keep doing the same thing. I remember attending a church where the pastor's wife and I were asked to help with the children's ministry. She was a public school teacher and very creative. We were excited about our project.

We began our new assignment by checking out the present way of teaching children on Sunday mornings. After entering a plain-looking room with no curtains or anything with color, we watched the few children sitting on chairs in a semi-circle while the teacher attempted to teach. She read half of her lesson in a very monotone voice. The children were fidgety, half-asleep, and obviously bored.

After spending several weeks painting, putting up brightly colored curtains, and establishing learning centers in several rooms, we were ready to begin. Within a few weeks, the attendance had grown so fast we had filled all the rooms. Children were excited and bringing all their friends to church.

Not everyone was excited, however. Many of the long time members of the church began complaining. "This is not the way we've done things before!" they said. Before long

---

When traditions fail to accept restored truth, the Lord finds people whose hearts are hungry. They become the new wineskin for revival.

---

we were asked to go back to the old method of teaching the children. Shortly after we did so, children's attendance dropped.

What happened? The old method of teaching worked many years before, but it did not work in the new season. When Moses crossed the Red Sea, God instructed him to use a rod to part the waters. Years later when the time came for Joshua to cross the Jordan River in order to enter the Promised Land, he knew that the old method would not work. Instead, Joshua had a multi-membered priesthood step into the Jordan and it parted. Using the rod of Moses would not have caused the

Jordan River to part. What worked in the old season would not work in the new.

Knowing the Times

The Church needs an Issachar anointing for this time of transition (1 Chron. 12:32). An understanding of this anointing is described in my book, *Prophetic Intercession* (Renew Books). The sons of Issachar understood God's strategic times and seasons. They had the wisdom to know what Israel should do during those times. We need an alert spirit during this time of transition so we know what we, as the Church, should do.

An Issachar anointing will help us recognize what is happening in the Church today. We will know that the Lord is bringing change to His Church. This is not a change created by a group of people, but rather is one that is orchestrated by the Lord. Traditions often fail to recognize when God is bringing the Church into a new season. Tradition wants to continue in the older more familiar ways of the Church.

Throughout church history, the old move has continually persecuted the new move of God. The Lord always offers the new to the last group who received His revival Spirit. Paul went to the Jews first. They had been the last people to receive the truth of God. When they refused the fresh revelation, Paul then took it to the Gentiles.

During the past century, God has offered restored truth to each group that was part of the previous move of His Spirit. This offer included the Pentecostals, Latter Rain, and charismatic churches. How sad that most of these churches held on to traditions and failed to embrace the fresh move of God's Spirit. When traditions fail to accept restored truth, the Lord finds people whose hearts are hungry. They become the new

wineskins for revival. God has churches today that have received the restoration of the new apostolic order. These
churches are the new wineskins.

A New Name on the Road to Success

Often, the new wineskins must receive a new identity. The
identity of the past season does not describe the church or
individual of the new season. Several years ago Pastor Robert Heidler of Denton, Texas, said the Lord had told him to
use a new name. Everyone knew him with the loving name of
"Pastor Hobie." Now he was to be called "Pastor Robert."
Why would the Lord tell him that? Wasn't his old name good
enough?

New Beginnings Church in Houston, Texas, recently
changed its name. The Lord spoke the new name: "Father's
House." The old name no longer identified the church nor the
focus of the ministry. The people needed a new name for the
new season.

In the Bible people often changed their names to identify
their new walk with the Lord. Abram became Abraham. Jacob
became Israel. Saul became Paul. Often the name change
spoke of a character change. Jacob, the supplanter, became
Israel, a prince with God. The new name was instrumental in
identifying the newly released destiny of God.

The Lord wants to speak a new name to people of the New
Order. The identity of the old season will keep a person in
captivity. The person will act out in life what he or she believes to be true of themselves. *"For as he thinks within
himself, so he is"* (Prov. 23:7). Therefore, the Lord desires to
speak to the potential in His people, not their present position
in life.

Jesus spoke to Peter and gave him a new identity. *"And Jesus said to him, 'Blessed are you, Simon Barjona, because flesh and blood did not reveal this to you, but My Father who is in heaven. I also say to you that you are Peter . . .'"* (Matt. 16:17-18). Simon would no longer be a shifting, unstable person. He was now Peter and was released into his potential. In the new season he would be a rock of stability and strength.

Let the Lord speak your new name to you. Although it may not literally be a new name, as in the case of Jacob or Peter, it will bring you out of captivity and into a new place of freedom. *"The nations will see your righteousness, and all kings your glory; And you will be called by a new name which the mouth of the Lord will designate"* (Isa. 62:2). Your old name may have been "failure." It may have been "desolate." Maybe your name was "abandoned." The Lord wants to remove the reproach of that name. His new name for you may be "successful." It may be "fruitful." How about the name "loved by God"? The new name He speaks will enable you to reach your destiny. It will empower you to help reach your neighbors. Your new identity will authorize you to help take cities and territories for the Lord!

Don't be surprised as you see churches change their names. The New Order is taking place today. The new name for an individual or for a church will set that person or congregation on the road to success.

Becoming a Risk-Taker

Many people in the old season have been people of fear. Fears of every description once controlled my life. The Lord had to set me free and give me a new name before I could embrace His call on my life. Today, I love trying new things. I love going new places and meeting new people. I love taking risks and seeing the Lord break through into the new season for my life.

People of the New Order are risk-takers. They are willing to step out of the familiar. They are willing to step out of their comfort zones. These people are full of faith in God. Even in tight places, they are able to see the Lord's hand. Tight places are used by the Lord to transition His people into the new place.

A butterfly may be uncomfortable in the cocoon. The little creature grows and changes in a tight place. However, breaking out of the tight place produces strength needed for the new place. No longer is the little creature limited to crawling on the ground as a worm. Now, a new day has dawned. A new order has been instituted. The worm has a new name. It is called a butterfly. The name describes its destiny. The potential for flying has become reality. The butterfly now takes risks and goes into unknown places. The tight place has squeezed the worm into the butterfly; the new place that God purposed. A transformation has taken place.

Transformation and Glory

The purpose of transition is transformation. God is restoring glory to His church. Many Bible scholars believe human beings were originally clothed like their Maker – in light and glory. When sin entered the garden, one of the things humanity lost was the glory. Jesus came to restore all that was lost. The restoration of glory is taking place in the Church today. Jesus took Peter, James, and John to a high mountain. As He stood before them, the disciples saw glory. *"And He was transfigured before them; and His face shone like the sun, and His garments became as white as light*" (Matt. 17:2). The glory they saw was a visible experience of kingdom power. The radiance they saw was not a reflection of light but a shining forth of God's glory. The transfiguration that took place is the Greek word *metamorphoo* from which we get the word metamorphosis—a transformation; a transfiguration.

The Church today is undergoing a transfiguration. As a result, the same release of glory is taking place in the Church as took place when Jesus was transfigured. The glory of the Lord is being released to fill the earth!

Today we are not who we will be tomorrow. A transformation is taking place. We are becoming the people God created us to be – a people of destiny; a people of the New Order.

Notes
[1] Michael Agnes, *Webster's New World College Dictionary* (New York, NY: Macmillan USA, 1999), p.1521.

CHAPTER THREE

THE APOSTOLIC CHURCH

Some children seem to come into this world with their minds made up. Our daughter Lori was one of those children. When she decided what she wanted, nothing could change her mind. As a small child, her favorite word was, "No!" She loved to pull all the food out of the pantry. Cans of vegetables, boxes of cereal, and bottles of mayonnaise or catsup were frequently strewn across the kitchen floor. Moving her to another room to try to distract her did not help. Attempts at various forms of discipline failed to stop her. She was what some people call a "strong-willed child."

I knew the determination I saw in her was a gift from God. Only it was hard to receive it as a gift at that stage in her life. The gift often seemed more like a curse. Her actions kept me praying for wisdom as a mother. I wanted to channel this gift into positive actions. How could I do this without breaking her will? It was a question I asked the Lord daily.

Today Lori still possesses the same traits. She makes up her mind and then perseveres until her goal is complete. The difference between her life today as an adult and as a child over 20 years ago is that she has submitted these same traits to the Lord. He uses the gift to get her through every difficult situation. She is unstoppable. No situation or emotion deters her. When Lori determines a goal, she stays focused and presses through until she reaches it.

Divine Determination

This determination in Lori is also seen in our heavenly Father. God is not always changing His mind. When He decides to do something, He continues until the goal is fulfilled. God is not like many people who change their minds frequently. Listening to many of them talk causes us to think that God changes His mind about His will for them on a daily basis. Today they may believe God wants them to go to a certain church. Tomorrow they may believe He wants them to attend another church. Then in only a matter of a few months they believe the Lord is "leading" them to another church. It seems as though God just can't make up His mind where He wants these people to be.

But God knows exactly what He wants, and He knows His will for His people who are having trouble hearing His will for their lives. The Lord has been working toward one purpose throughout eternity. He has never changed His mind. Fleeting thoughts or some spirit of adventure does not motivate Him. He is only motivated by His divine plan. His plan is to bring glory to Himself forever. God has a plan for people who will be His Church. It is not for a religious organization. His plan is for people who will adequately represent Him on earth and be His agent for transformation.

A People of Destiny

God's people, the Church, will reveal the wisdom and power of God to the forces of darkness and wickedness. *"So that the manifold wisdom of God might now be made known through the church to the rulers and the authorities in the heavenly places"* (Eph. 3:10). The many features of wisdom and power will be evident in the people of the New Order. They will have hearts to see lives and cities transformed, and understand that they are not accidents or mistakes, but are instead a people of destiny. Their lives are the very plan of God.

Before He put stars in the sky, hung the moon in place, set galaxies on their courses, or created the earth, God planned for the lives of His people. It is with this understanding that they realize they have come into the Kingdom *"for such a time as this"* (Esther 4:14).

Keys to Unlocking Territories and Peoples

The Lord has commissioned apostolic people to go into all the world and disciple every people group. His people realize that the scope of this commission includes their own neighborhoods, cities, and places of employment.

The assignment of the Lord is beyond those who preach behind pulpits. How then do these people accomplish God's plan for their lives? The Lord has given several keys to unlocking territories and peoples that have been locked in darkness by the enemy.

1. A Burden for the Lost

One of the keys available to the apostolic church is prayer and intercession. Apostolic people intercede. The prayers, however, are not only for personal needs. They have a burden for the lost. They cry out for the Lord to be glorified in their cities and places of business.

During the '70s and '80s, the Church received much revelation about God's name as Jehovah Jireh. Teachers expounded on Scriptures revealing God's will to bless His people. He is the God who *"shall supply all our needs according to His riches in glory in Christ Jesus"* (Phil. 4:19). That truth will never change. God is a covenant-keeping God. When we walk in covenant with Him, He provides for us. However, we are not to stop with having our own needs met. The heart of God is one who loves and gives to others. God's heart is for the whole earth to walk in covenant with Him. All nations will acknowledge His lordship.

Apostolic churches have a passion to see their families and neighbors worship the Lord. They are willing to pray and

---

The Lord delights in using ordinary
individuals for His purposes. The humility
in the heart of an ordinary person releases
the power of an extraordinary God!

---

intercede for the lost. As a result of intercession, hearts are softened and become receptive to the gospel. In prayer the Lord speaks strategy for reaching people. Empowering for transformation begins in the prayer room.

Those who received the Great Commission during Jesus' time on earth were ordinary believers. They had no political, social, or economic influence. They were, however, instrumental in changing the course of history. Jesus told His followers to become witnesses in their own city, Jerusalem. The assignment began in a prayer meeting in the Upper Room. As the people were obedient to pray, hear from the Lord, and receive empowerment during prayer, their cities and regions experienced revival. However, the revival did not stop with their cities, but it poured out to all the known world of that day. *"They were continually devoting themselves to the apostles' teaching and to fellowship, to the breaking of bread and to prayer"* (Acts 2:42). *"This took place for two years, so that all who lived in Asia heard the word of the Lord, both Jews and Greeks"* (Acts 19:10).

2. A Passion for Revival

After 2,000 years, we are still experiencing the impact of the Upper Room prayer meeting. The task is not impossible. God is able to unlock entire regions, as homes throughout an area become houses of prayer. As individuals dedicate their homes as houses of prayer, revival fires will begin to burn throughout the land.

Sue Curran wrote in her book, *The Praying Church*, about the results of a few individuals who began to pray. These praying individuals helped ignite a worldwide revival. "Revival historians call the year 1858-1859 the Annus Mirabulus-Year of Miracles. The countries of Japan, China, and India all opened to the Gospel through treaties with Great Britain. This was the great revival that spawned men, movements, and missions as never before. Dwight Moody, Andrew Murray, and William Booth received their great impetus at this time. The Salvation Army was born, and Hudson Taylor's China Inland Mission reported an increase in conversions of

25 percent.

"It began with one man who called a few other business-men together for prayer on their lunch hour in New York. Within six months ten thousand or more men in New York City alone were praying at the noon hour. A traveling man mentioned that he found a prayer meeting that extended from Omaha to New York."[1]

3. Prayer That Transforms a Region

Prayer is a key to seeing an entire region come into transfor-mation. Throughout history, cities and territories have experienced change as a result of prayer. The region Gideon lived in was in great need of transformation. The Midianite desert warriors invaded the northern Israelite farm country every year around harvest time to take whatever they could. These raiders eventually forced farmers to abandon their fields and look for safety in caves or other mountain strong-holds. Gideon sought safety in a wine press while he threshed grain by hand rather than with oxen and sledge in a hilltop field.

Gideon was a member of the Abiezrite clan, the weakest in the tribe of Manasseh. He seemed to be the least likely person to overcome such powerful enemies. Nevertheless, he was God's choice. The Lord delights in using ordinary individuals for His purposes. The humility in the heart of an ordinary person releases the power of an extraordinary God! Gideon was a man of humility. He sought the will of the Lord in several ways before confronting the enemy.

As Gideon conversed with the Lord, God spoke strategy for defeating the enemy. Gideon was obedient to follow the instructions he heard from the Lord in prayer. As a result of fervent prayer and obedience, the region Gideon lived in was transformed. *"So Midian was subdued before the sons of Israel, and they did not lift up their heads anymore. And the land was undisturbed for forty years in the days of Gideon"* (Judges 8:28).

An apostolic church is a praying church. The apostolic churches pray corporately. Prayer is in their homes. People of the New Order are people who live a lifestyle of prayer—prayer powerful enough to transform regions.

4. Worship and Intercession

A characteristic of the New Order is that worship and intercession are mingled together. Apostolic churches stand at the Altar of Incense. The flow of worship and intercession is unbroken. As they worship, the heart of the Father is revealed. Out of the Father's heart, they intercede. After praying the will of the Lord, they flow back into worship and praise to the Lord. Heaven and earth are joined together in one unbroken symphony.

Worship is more than singing Christian songs. Worship involves the invitation for the Lord of hosts to overcome the powers of evil on the earth. At the invitation of the Church, the Lord is binding the forces of darkness and allowing the lost to be receptive to the gospel. People then receive the Lord in great numbers. As a result of God's presence in the lives of many people in a city, laws in that city change. Occult activity, immoral business, and crime are drastically reduced. The city begins to transform.

5. Focused Vision

Not only do apostolic churches pray, they also have a focused vision. Several years ago I noticed my eyesight started to change. Print that had been clear in the past was no longer clear. I had to strain my eyes to be able to see small print. The number six sometimes looked like the number eight. When making phone calls, I would dial the wrong number because my vision was not clear.

After obtaining reading glasses, I was amazed at how much clearer things became. I could see details that I had not seen before. Rather than seeing just a vague image, I was able to see every aspect of a picture. Likewise, our spiritual vision must be focused. There are many good things for us to do, yet the Church must stay focused on winning the lost and seeing change come to cities.

6. Taking Ownership of a City

The Church has often considered heaven as home and the earth as just a place to endure. Scriptures have been used to justify the earth as Satan's territory. *"In whose case the god of this world has blinded the minds of the unbelieving so that they might not see the light of the gospel of the glory of Christ, who is the image of God"* (2 Cor. 4:4). But apostolic churches realize that the earth belongs to the Lord. They are the managers of the Lord's earth. *"The earth is the Lord's, and all it contains, the world, and those who dwell in it"* (Ps. 24:1).

With this understanding, apostolic churches have a burden for possessing the land. I remember a few brief times when my husband and I rented houses. While living in those houses, we did not put new roofs on them, install new carpet, or make major repairs. The reason we did not do these things was because the houses did not belong to us. On the other hand, in all the houses we have owned over the past 35 years, we have always had a new roof put on when the old one leaked. New carpet was always installed when the old carpet was worn. We repaired whatever was in need of it. The reason was because we owned those houses. We take care of the things we own.

The same thing happens in a city. When we have a revelation of owning a city, we take care of the city. Apostolic churches are concerned about evil government. These churches care about the kind of education found in the schools. Neighbors and neighborhoods are important. God has put His church in the city and given it responsibility as His stewards. As apostolic churches, we must become involved in our cities.

Since we own the city, we are to serve the city. Several years ago I arrived to minister at a church in a town in Texas. Due to lack of funds, the city had announced they were closing the only hospital in that town. Residents would be required to drive a long distance for the services of a hospital. The pastor at the church heard the news. Because he had taken ownership of his city in his heart, he was determined to serve the town.

The pastor met with other pastors in the city. They enlisted the members of their churches for several citywide fund-raisers. Finances poured in. As a result of their efforts, the city officials kept the hospital open. The churches of that city did not boycott certain businesses nor did they picket in front of the government offices. They served the city. Out of a heart of loving and serving, God gave them favor. The entire city realized the churches were responsible for helping. A new favor came upon the churches. People were more open to the gospel. Greatness in the kingdom of God comes out of a heart of servitude.

7. A Heart for Unity

Apostolic churches have a heart for unity. Pastor Glen in

Florida recently told me a story about the churches in his city. For years the churches in that area have been divided. Each church would hold its own services and show little concern for the others. Despite the division, Pastor Glen had been reaching out to encourage other pastors. He did not have his own agenda in doing this. He simply wanted to get to know them. He met some of the pastors through divine appointments. One of them he met on a plane.

As a result of Pastor Glen's reaching out, a regular meeting for prayer and fellowship is now attended by Baptist, Pentecostal, Lutheran, African, Cuban, and Presbyterian pastors. He doesn't know how to explain what has happened. The Lord sovereignly put a desire in the hearts of these pastors to know one another and be a unified church in the city. Occasionally, joint services are held. The members of these churches are walking in a spirit of love and unity. The city is seeing the reality of Jesus in His Body. *"By this all men will know that you are My disciples, if you have love for one another"* (John 13:35). Apostolic churches walk in unity.

8. Apostles and Prophets Linked Together

Another characteristic of apostolic churches is found in leadership. Often you see apostles and prophets linked together in ministry. The Bible records the success of cities that are transformed through the leadership of the apostles and prophets. Those cities carry a breakthrough anointing. God has given them an ability to breakthrough the spiritual forces of darkness so a group of people or an area has the power to move into a new place.

An example of the apostolic and prophetic anointing is in the book of Haggai. Zerubbabel was the appointed governor. In the Old Testament, governors, kings, and rulers were types of apostles. The temple had not been completely restored. The people were in a state of apathy. The Lord sent the prophet Haggai to the city alongside Zerubbabel. Through their combined efforts, the temple was restored.

Apostolic churches embrace apostles and prophets. For these churches to complete the task the Lord has given them, they need these ministries linked together. Apostles and prophets become a dynamic team to break opposition against the Lord's purposes. Apostolic churches are able to be successful in areas where others in the past have experienced defeat.

Maintaining Success

Success, however, must be maintained. The enemy does not stop when he experiences a setback. He looks for an opportunity to gain ground once again. Apostolic churches are not ignorant of the devices of the enemy. *"So that no advantage would be taken of us by Satan, for we are not ignorant of his schemes"* (2 Cor. 2:11). For this reason, apostolic churches maintain alertness in the spirit. Purity of heart is a priority. Holiness marks the life of these believers. There is an intense desire to be transformed into the likeness of the Lord. Passion for God consumes these believers. They do not rest in past victories. These churches are always attentive for any openings to the enemy. Grateful for the entirety of what the Lord has done in the past, they press on until their lives and cities become a praise to the Lord in all the earth!

Notes
[1] Sue Curran, *The Praying Church*, (Ventura, CA: Regal Books, 1999), pp. 115-116.

CHAPTER FOUR

PEOPLE OF THE NEW ORDER

Tiffany Ramsey is one of my "spiritual daughters." Her mother, Brenda, is the International Prayer Coordinator for our ministry. Tiffany has experienced the miracle-working power of God in her life. She was born with a cleft palate. After multiple surgeries and years of speech therapy, the doctors told her parents she would never be able to speak normally. But God!

The Lord has healed Tiffany so completely that she sings with one of the most beautiful, professional voices of anyone I have ever heard. She knows she has a call of God on her life and has ministered in many nations of the world. She is also aware that the Lord has called her as a person of the New Order. She is not sitting around waiting for some great door of opportunity to open. She understands she is called to minister wherever the Lord places her.

A Light in the Workplace

After graduating from Bible school and college, Tiffany went to work in Dallas for a large telecommunications company. She recognizes that God placed her there, and she is called as a light in the corporate workplace. It did not take long before her coworkers saw something different in Tiffany's life. They saw she had a purpose for living, a love for people, and a peace and hope they did not have. Several people asked her what made her different. She was happy to tell them about the miracle in her life. She also told them about her personal relationship with Jesus Christ.

The inquirers then wanted to know if Tiffany would teach them the Bible and show them how to have a relationship with the Lord. They loved the fruit in Tiffany's life and wanted it for themselves.

Tiffany went to her supervisor and asked for the use of a meeting room for the lunch hour one day each week. Since Tiffany is an excellent employee and the favor of God is on her, she was given permission. People in her work place be-

---

◆

[People of the New Order] are not observers of ministry. They are participants.

◆

---

gan attending the weekly Bible studies. They have been receiving Jesus as their Savior, filled with the Holy Spirit, and experiencing healing and deliverance. The Bible study is now a company recognized Employee Special Interest Group entitled "Ambassadors For Christ."

Soon some of Tiffany's coworkers asked her if they could meet an extra day each week for prayer and ministry. After receiving permission, some in the group began meeting for weekly prayer meetings. Several months later, Ed Silvoso scheduled a Light the Nation conference in Dallas. Before the conference, Tiffany took Ambassadors For Christ out on the streets of Dallas to go on prayerwalks and hand out tracts during lunch breaks. Most had never heard of doing such things. By the end of the prayerwalk, even the most reluctant ones were excited to serve the Lord in such a way.

By the time the group had met for one year, the meeting space was overflowing. After Tiffany's request for a larger room, the building manager refused. It did not take long before the Lord transferred the manager to another building and replaced him. *"He removes kings and establishes kings;"* (Dan. 2:21).

The new building manager gave Tiffany one of the largest meeting rooms available, which happens to be the most beautiful corporate meeting room. She has been given permission to put flyers and announcements all over the building advertising the Bible studies and ministry times.

The good report has spread throughout downtown Dallas. Many from other businesses have heard how people's lives are being changed, and they are coming on their lunch breaks to attend Ambassadors For Christ. As a result, many others are starting Bible studies.

Tiffany understands she is a person of the New Order. Ministry is for more than the few people who preach from a pulpit in a church building. Every believer is a minister. She is the "pastor" at this telecommunications company. They provide a building for her to meet and a congregation for her ministry. They even pay her salary!

Characteristics of
New Order People

What makes Tiffany different from the traditional church member? What are some characteristics of these New Order people? It is apparent with these people that they view the Church in a radically different way than their predecessors. The empowerment of the Holy Spirit in their lives is for ministry to a lost world. They are not *observers* of ministry. They are *participants*.

1. They "Hear The Sound"

One of the characteristics of people of the New Order is that they hear a sound before they see a manifestation. They have prophetic vision and prophetic ears. These people sense the direction the Lord is taking His people before they see it fully manifested in the earth.

Elijah was such a person. He heard the sound of rain before he could see the evidence. *"Now Elijah said to Ahab, 'Go up, eat and drink; for there is the sound of the roar of a heavy shower'"* (1 Kings 18:41). He sent his servant to look seven times before the rain clouds were visible.

On the day of Pentecost, the sound of wind was heard before the visible tongues of fire. *"And suddenly there came from heaven a noise like a violent, rushing wind, and it filled the whole house where they were sitting. And there appeared to them tongues as of fire distributing themselves, and they rested on each one of them"* (Acts 2:2-3).

2. They Have Prophetic Sight

New Order people live in the reality of the future. Not only have they heard a fresh sound from heaven, but they have a prophetic anointing to see the future moves of God before they are materialized fully in the earth. Dr. Bill Hamon describes this spiritual ability:

"I believe that the anointed ability of restorational prophets is similar to the equipment that astronomers have to look into far distant space. They can see things numerous light-years away. They are developing newer and greater ways to see with greater clarity farther distances away. The prophets and apostles are developing new and greater ways to see into the distant future. The prophets spoke of the coming of the Messiah Movement hundreds of thousands of years before it was manifest on earth. They did not know the what, how and when, but they did know that it was coming."[1]

3. They Allow the Lord to Position Them

New Order people are not necessarily apostles or prophets, but they possess apostolic and prophetic anointings. They are willing to follow the leading of the Lord into uncharted waters. They have a desire to be positioned in the place where the Lord can use them to help bring forth a great harvest. Therefore, they allow the Lord to position them as instruments of harvest for His kingdom purposes.

Ruth was a type of New Order person. She was willing to leave the comforts of her traditional background. She heard the sound of harvest and was willing to be repositioned. *"Then she arose with her daughters-in-law that she might return from the land of Moab, for she had heard in the land of Moab that the Lord had visited His people in giving them food"* (Ruth 1:6).

The new positioning involves moving from a "lay person" mentality to a "minister" mentality. That means you must be able to see the harvest field in the place God has chosen for you. The harvest field may be at the grocery store. It may be at the bank, office, gas station, your child's soccer practice, or in your neighborhood. The harvest field is wherever you are. You are not there for the obvious reasons. You are there because the Lord has positioned you in that place for His purposes.

4. They Have a Team Spirit

Another characteristic of people of the New Order is that they have a team spirit. Although they have individual anointings and giftings, they see themselves as part of a team. Jesus gave us a model to follow. He sent His disciples out two by two as they ministered (Luke 10:1). New Order people are not independent but are, rather, interdependent. The leadership of their local churches has activated them. They see themselves as an extension of this team.

God has put team spirit in His creation. A visible picture of this spirit can be seen in geese flying in "V" formation. An individual bird flapping his wings causes uplift for the bird following. If a goose falls out of formation, a drag and resistance takes place by trying to fly alone. When the lead goose gets tired, he rotates back in the "V" formation and another goose flies point. The geese honk from behind to encourage those up front to keep up the speed. If a goose gets sick or wounded by gunshot and falls out of formation, two other geese fall out and lend help or protection until the bird is restored.

What a picture of a team! Paul described the same principle in Ephesians: *"From whom the whole body, being fitted and held together by what every joint supplies, according to the proper working of each individual part, causes the growth of the body for the building up of itself in love"* (Eph. 4:16).

Every person (joint) is necessary in the body. The joints (people) are fitted together as a team and will produce growth in the body.

5. They Have Servants' Hearts

The "team" frequently functions outside church buildings. Churches in the city are considered part of the team. The heart of a servant motivates people of the New Order. They are not looking for titles but are interested in *function*. These people have a desire to build the kingdom of God rather than building their own kingdom. Jesus had this same heart. He deserved to be served, but He chose to serve others. *"If I then, the Lord and the Teacher, washed your feet, you also ought to wash one another's feet"* (John 13:14).

The husband of one of my friends died recently. As pastors of a church, they had developed a good relationship with other churches in the area. When the churches in town heard about the death, several of them volunteered to bring and serve food on the day of the funeral. This involved feeding several hundred people! Doctrine, style of worship, church government, or spiritual gifts were not issues. These churches view themselves as part of a team called to build the kingdom of God in that city. New Order people have servants' hearts.

6. They Pray With Authority

One aspect of serving is through intercession. Intercessors have a passion to see transformation in neighborhoods or cities. Prayer time is not limited to a certain place or a particular style. Many people pray with groups of intercessors from other churches. Some cities have groups meeting monthly. The meetings rotate to different churches under different leadership. The meetings exist for one purpose – to see the lost in their city come to salvation.

We will find the intercessors praying in the grocery store, work place, restaurants, or any place they go. It is not unusual to find them in all-night prayer meetings. A few years ago, most churches would not announce a "prayer meeting." The leaders knew that hardly anyone would show up. Now, prayer meetings draw larger crowds than most other special meetings in the churches.

Not only do New Order people love to pray, they sense an authority in their prayers. They have an understanding from Scripture that they are God's representatives in the earth. As His representatives, they speak as with His voice. Prophetic intercession, proclamations, declarations, and prophetic songs are an integral part of the prayer life.

Recently I was part of a team of ministers speaking at a conference in Waco, Texas. The conference theme was "Seize the City." Intercessors gathered for several days to hear how they could bring their city under the lordship of Jesus. On one of the prayerwalks to historically strategic sites, we crossed a bridge over a river. About halfway across the bridge, an intercessor faced the city and cried out loudly, "Waco, hear the word of the Lord!" She then made prophetic proclamations about the will of the Lord for that city. The other intercessors verbally agreed by shouting, "Yes! Amen! Do it, Lord!" A sense that the proclamations were not merely the words of a human being came upon the team. God had spoken prophetically through one of His representatives.

7. They Guard Against Evil

When the Lord placed man and woman in the Garden of Eden, He gave them responsibility. The responsibility included watching over the garden and guarding it against any intrusion of evil. God has not changed His mind. New Order people have received the same assignment for their cities. Therefore, they are willing to investigate openings in their cities that have allowed evil to enter. They are alert to guard and pray so they can help dismantle strongholds. Research and study to uncover strongholds in areas is common.

Harold Caballeros explains the necessity of the research, known as spiritual mapping:

"When a territory has been inhabited by persons who have chosen to offer their worship to demons, the land has been contaminated and those territorial spirits have obtained a right to remain there, keeping the inhabitants captive. It is then necessary to identify the enemy and to go into spiritual battle, until we obtain victory and redeem the territory. Spiritual mapping is a means toward identifying the enemy. It is our spiritual espionage."[2]

8. They Are World-Changers

Seeing transformation in their territory is a vision of New Order people. Their lives are not destined for the ordinary. The Lord has destined them to help reshape the world in which they live.

Ann Lattimore is a world-changer. She and her husband plant and oversee churches in small towns. Yet, she has a heart for Houston, Texas, the city where she lives. After hearing of what Tiffany Ramsey was doing in Dallas, Ann asked the Lord, "How do I reach this city?"

He answered, "One building at a time." As Ann looked at the skyline of the city, she saw many tall skyscrapers. Up to 40,000 people spend at least eight hours a day, five days a week in each of those buildings. The population of one building is as large as a small town. Now she had her answer. Ann had business opportunities in many of those buildings—opportunities that could now be used for the kingdom of God. Ann began a Bible study in one of the skyscrapers. When the Bible study grew and had a leader, she would start a Bible study in another building. Now there are Bible studies in buildings all over the city. She is reaching her city "one building at a time." Ann believes she can help change her world.

A mandate as world-changers propels New Order people out of mediocrity and into a life of challenges and opportunities. Like Abraham, they have the promise of a great inheritance. Like Moses, they believe they are living to deliver a people out of bondage. Like the apostle Paul, they *". . . press on toward the goal for the prize of the upward call of God in Christ Jesus"* (Phil. 3:14).

Notes

[1] Dr. Bill Hamon, *Apostles, Prophets and the Coming Moves of God* (Shippensburg, PA: Destiny Image, 1997), p. 239.

[2] Harold Caballeros, "Defeating the Enemy With the Help of Spiritual Mapping," *Breaking Strongholds in Your City*, C. Peter Wagner, ed. (Ventura, CA: Regal Books, 1993), p. 145.

CHAPTER FIVE

SUPERNATURAL SAINTS

Since 1994 I have had the joy of working with apostle Dexter Low in Malaysia. Dexter has planted indigenous churches throughout Malaysia since 1976. Malaysia is located in an area known as the 10/40 Window, the least evangelized part of the world. In spite of the hindrances, Dexter and his churches are changing the statistics!

The Healing of a Witch Doctor

At the 1998 annual convention for the Latter Rain apostolic network, members of the churches gave testimonies. Several people shared about the work of the Lord in their villages in East Malaysia. One lady told the story of a witch doctor in her village. He was paralyzed. None of his followers had been able to restore him to health. The lady told how she went to visit him and asked him to let her pray for healing. After laying hands on the paralyzed witch doctor, he was totally healed! He then wanted to know about this Jesus who healed him.

The praying lady was not the pastor or a minister from the Latter Rain church. She was a tiny, 95-pound member of the congregation. The members of those churches are taught that they can lay hands on the sick and see them healed. They know that the Lord uses signs and wonders to get the attention of unbelievers. They are not to be afraid of the power of the enemy but are to have faith in the power of God.

Arising With Power

Most Christians fail to find fulfillment in experiencing the Holy Spirit's empowerment for ministry. In reality, far too many of God's children function below the potential available to them. They have accepted an *ordinary* walk with the Lord when He has made the *extraordinary* available. The heavenly dynamic of signs and wonders can operate *naturally* through the believer and release him or her into *supernatural* manifestations of the life and works of Jesus.

Believers are starting to arise with God's power operating in their lives. Church leaders are now teaching, training, and activating the members to minister in the power of the Holy Spirit. In the past, ministry through church members was not the norm for traditional churches in the United States and other countries. The pastor was expected to visit the sick, pray, preach, teach, keep everyone happy, and sometimes was even the janitor for the building. The congregation was there to sing when told to sing and sit when told to sit. After leaving the weekly service, they felt they had pleased God. Not anymore! The Holy Spirit is activating the Church for ministry.

After being filled with the Holy Spirit in 1974, I received

an incredible hunger for the Bible. Hours were spent each day devouring the Scriptures. During this time, I read about the Early Church in the book of Acts. I noticed signs and wonders were normal for believers. They were not in my life even though I had been a believer since the age of 12.

Immediately I began to pray for the manifestation of power I had read about in the Early Church. I thought I must not be full of the Holy Spirit if signs and wonders were not part of my life. If someone had told me differently, I may not have pressed into the Lord. Why had I not understood my role of ministry as a believer in all those years I spent attending church?

In his book *Churchquake*, Dr. C. Peter Wagner discusses the acceptance of lay ministry:

"The apostolic theology of lay ministry is a fairly recent discovery in church history-namely, a discovery of the past 25 or 30 years. We do not find this in Martin Luther or John Calvin or John Wesley or other classic theologians, either Protestant or Catholic. There was some of this in the British Plymouth Brethren Movement and some in the U.S. Restoration Movement led by Alexander Campbell and Barton Stone and some in fringe movements here and there. However, it did not mainstream into the Body of Christ, at least in the United States, until the publication of Ray Stedman's book *Body Life* (Regal Books) in 1972. This was the first widely recognized and accepted biblical theology of lay ministry, although written in a popular style."[1]

A New Day for Lay Ministry

Many churches today conduct schools of ministry or hold training sessions for their members. Thousands of believers fill conference rooms for prophetic or apostolic seminars. Many travel great distances to attend conferences that will equip them to minister. These people are not "spooky" Christians. They are normal believers seeking to do what the Bible says they should be doing.

In his book *Experiencing the Spirit*, Robert Heidler encourages believers to develop spiritual gifts for ministry:

"When it comes to the gifts of the Holy Spirit, many Christians think, *Some people have them. Some people don't. It's God's choice, and there's nothing we can do.* They assume that if you don't have a powerful gifting now, you may as well sit back and leave the job of ministry to those who do. But, that's not what the Bible says about spiritual gifts.

"The Bible describes the functioning of the gifts as a process of growth. We are encouraged to stir up and exercise the gifts we have (see 2 Tim. 1:6), to pray for and seek additional gifts and to impart spiritual gifts from one believer to another. We should be developing proficiency in using more and more of the Spirit's gifts so we can be more and more effective in serving Jesus."[2]

Apostles are helping to activate apostolic people. The distinguishing marks of an apostle are signs and wonders. Apostolic people operate in an anointing similar to the apostle. *"The signs of a true apostle were performed among you with all perseverance, by signs and wonders and miracles"* (2 Cor. 12:12). Therefore, apostolic people have an anointing for signs and wonders. The potential is available for every believer.

Our Potential for Signs and Wonders

God puts potential in creatures He has created. The moment a bird is born it manifests every bird-like faculty and characteristic. The small creature eats, breathes, moves, and thinks like a bird. Later, it spreads its wings, takes to the air, and flies like a bird. The offspring of birds can fly and sing. The reason they can do this is because they have the nature of a bird.

The offspring of humans cannot fly. They have the wrong nature. However, God has provided a reproduction of His divine nature in His children. We are able to exhibit supernatural abilities since we have the nature of Father God, who is supernatural.

God has given His children great potential for signs and wonders. *"Behold, I and the children whom the Lord has given me are for signs and wonders in Israel from the Lord of hosts, who dwells on Mount Zion"* (Isa. 8:18). We are created for signs and wonders!

What are signs and wonders? The word *sign* in the Greek language is the word *semeion.* Signs are like fingers pointing to God. They lead to something out of and beyond themselves. They are "valuable not so much for what they are as for what they indicate of the grace and power of the doer or his immediate connection with a higher spiritual world."[3]

Jesus operated in signs and wonders throughout His time on the earth. When He was in a boat with His disciples, a storm came up and the waters were rough. These disciples were experienced fishermen, and they knew the dangers involved with the storm. After Jesus rebuked the storm, the wind and waves ceased. His power over the storm was a sign to the disciples. Jesus then rebuked the disciples for their unbelief and lack of faith. *"They said to one another, 'Who then is this, that even the wind and the sea obey Him?'"* (Mark 4:41) Signs are often used to cause an unbeliever to be drawn to the Lord.

The word *wonders* is the Greek word *teras.* *"Teras*; often associated with *semeion*, sign, and usually translated as 'wonder.' These two words refer not to different classes of miracles, but to different qualities of the same miracle. *Teras* is derived from *tereo*, to watch, as being that which for its extraordinary character is apt to be observed and kept in the memory. It is a miracle regarded as startling, imposing, amazing."[4]

Tools to Win the Lost

Healing, deliverance, and signs and wonders frequently are released by the Lord to gain the attention of unbelievers. These are tools the evangelist uses to point people to the Lord Jesus. In his book *Power Evangelism*, John Wimber quotes C. Peter Wagner on this topic:

"When the gospel first penetrates a region, if we don't go in with an understanding of and use of the supernatural power of the Holy Spirit, we just don't make much headway....[For example,] in Brazil 40 percent of the population are practicing spiritists and another 40 percent have had some direct experience with it. The way the gospel is spreading there is by confrontation; healings, miracles, signs, and wonders."[5]

These same tools that the evangelists use are available to believers. John White seems to agree in his book, *When the Spirit Comes With Power*:

"I would define power evangelism as that sort of evangelism where the unsaved are compelled to pay attention by unmistakable evidence that a God of supernatural power is present. . . . Commonly in Jesus' day they were healings, including the healing of demoniacs. On the day of Pentecost it was the public spectacle of ignorant men speaking in known languages. At certain points in history it has been the stunning nature of radical conversions en masse."[6]

The Bible promises that God will touch people in ungodly societies through signs and wonders. *"Or has a god tried to go to take for himself a nation from within another nation by trials, by signs and wonders and by war and by a mighty hand and by an outstretched arm and by great terrors, as the Lord your God did for you in Egypt before your eyes?"* (Deut. 4:34). God delivered the nation of Israel out of Egypt through signs and wonders. He then delivers for Himself a "holy nation" (1 Peter 2:9) out of the nation of darkness through signs and wonders.

John G. Lake was a man powerfully used by the Lord. Hundreds of thousands of people were converted under his ministry. A story is told of one of his meetings in Pretoria, South Africa. It sounds similar to meetings taking place today:

"On Monday night the church was again packed to the doors. All available standing room was taken. The news had spread throughout the city. Many had come out of mere curiosity. A great company of the rougher elements of the city filled the standing space around the door. They were crowded shoulder to shoulder.

"I was in the act of preaching when suddenly the Spirit of God fell on the thickest of the group near the door, and a dozen men fell across one another in a heap under the power. Their friends were so amazed that they rushed from the church. Others caught their friends by the arms and literally dragged them out of the church. Some they even carried to the clubrooms across the street, and in their ignorance tried to revive them by pouring whiskey down their throats. Many were saved and baptized in the Spirit that night. The meeting broke up about daylight."[7]

The nations today are not just located in some other country of the world. They are found in our neighborhoods. These nations are in our cities. Churches are recognizing the mission fields located in their own geographical regions. Pastors are reporting results that sound like the day of Pentecost. As John Wimber reported:

"The blind see; the lame walk; the deaf hear. Cancer is disappearing. Most importantly for me as a pastor, the people are taking healing and other supernatural gifts to the streets, leading many who otherwise would not be open to the message of the gospel to Christ. I estimate that twenty percent of our people regularly see someone healed through their prayers. The gifts are not confined to church services; they are tools employed in reaching the lost."[8]

New Levels of Faith

God is filling His people with new levels of faith. This faith gives them the courage to minister to their neighbors. They are willing to pray for gang members, those involved in occult activity, and those who are members of false religions. Faith has replaced the former fear of reaching out and ministering to these individuals.

"If you should say in your heart, 'These nations are greater than I; how can I dispossess them?' you shall not be afraid of them; you shall well remember what the Lord your God did to Pharaoh and to all Egypt: the great trials which your eyes saw and the signs and the wonders and the mighty hand and the outstretched arm by which the Lord your God brought you out. So shall the Lord your God do to all the peoples of whom you are afraid" (Deut. 7:17-19).

The Lord is honoring faith and boldness. He is demonstrating His power to unbelievers through signs and wonders.

People who once frightened us now are hungry for the Lord. Their lives are being set in order by the power of God.

Apostles are being used to bring order. Apostolic people use signs and wonders to bring order out of disorder. Sick and broken bodies are brought in order through the healing power of Jesus. Tormented minds are set in order as captives are set free. The Spirit of God transforms ungodly lives. Cities are brought in order as great numbers of these people are converted and live godly lives.

Believers are being activated and empowered for harvest. God's power is being released in them to help gather the greatest harvest of souls in the history of the Church. They will say like the apostle Paul, *"And my message and my preaching were not in persuasive words of wisdom, but in demonstration of the Spirit and of power, so that your faith would not rest on the wisdom of men, but on the power of God"* (1 Cor. 2:4-5).

Notes

[1] C. Peter Wagner, *Churchquake* (Ventura, CA: Regal Books, 1999), p.211.

[2] Robert Heidler, *Experiencing the Spirit* (Ventura, CA: Renew Books, 1998), p.146.

[3] Spiros Zodhiates, *Hebrew-Greek Key Study Bible-New American Standard* (Chattanooga, TN: AMG Publishers, 1984; revised edition, 1990), p.1874.

[4] Ibid., p.1881.

[5] John Wimber with Kevin Springer, *Power Evangelism* (San Francisco, CA: Harper & Row, 1986), pp. 39-40.

[6] John White, *When the Spirit Comes With Power* (Downers Grove, Ill.: Intervarsity Press, 1988), p. 181.

[7] John G. Lake, *His Life, His Sermons, His Boldness of Faith* (Ft. Worth, TX: Kenneth Copeland Publications, 1994), p. 301.

[8] Wimber, p. 44.

Wagner Publications Presents:

RIDDING YOUR HOME OF SPIRITUAL DARKNESS
Chuck D. Pierce & Rebecca Wagner Sytsema

Christians are often completely unaware of how the enemy has gained access to their homes through what they own. This practical, easy-to-read book can be used by any Christian to pray through their home and property in order to close the door to the enemy and experience richer spiritual life. Included are chapters on children, sin, generational curses, and spiritual discernment, as well as a step-by-step guide to praying through your home and a section of questions and answers.
Paperback (75 pp.) • 0.9667481.7.4 • **$7.20 (save 10%)**

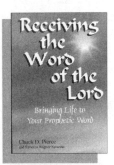

RECEIVING THE WORD OF THE LORD
Chuck D. Pierce & Rebecca Wagner Sytsema

The Bible makes it very clear that God has a plan for our lives. By hearing and receiving the voice of God, we can know our purpose and destiny. In this book you will discover how to hear the voice of God, develop an understanding of prophecy, learn how to test a prophetic word, and experience the joy of responding to God's voice.
Paperback (41 pp.) • 0.9667481.2.3 • **$5.40 (save 10%)**

From C. Peter Wagner . . .

RADICAL HOLINESS FOR RADICAL LIVING
C. Peter Wagner

Can anyone really live a holy life? Is there a test of holiness? *Radical Holiness for Radical Living* answers these and other questions as it opens the way for you to move to new levels in your Christian life. You can defeat Satan's schemes and enjoy daily victory in your walk with God.
Paperback (41 pp.) · 0.9667481.1.5 · **$5.40 (save 10%)**

HARD-CORE IDOLATRY: FACING THE FACTS
C. Peter Wagner

This hard-hitting book is destined to clear away the foggy thinking about idolatry that has permeated churches today. This book will help you recognize idolatry (even in some of our churches), confront the schemes of the enemy with more understanding and power, feel the pain of God's broken heart when His people worship idols, and begin to cleanse your home of idolatrous objects.
Paperback (43 pp.) · 0.9667481.4.X · **$5.40 (save 10%)**

REVIVAL! IT CAN TRANSFORM YOUR CITY
C. Peter Wagner

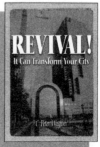

This book answers many questions including: What exactly is revival? Can my city actually be transformed through revival? What steps can be taken to sustain revival in a city? Discover how the Spirit of God can visibly transform our cities through the revival for which we have been praying!
Paperback (63 pp.) · 0.9667481.8.2 · **$5.40 (save 10%)**

HOW TO CAST OUT DEMONS: A BEGINNER'S GUIDE

Doris M. Wagner

Many modern Christians are now agreeing that we should take Jesus' command to cast out demons more seriously than we have. But how do we do it? Where do we start? This practical, down-to-earth book, written by a respected deliverance practitioner, will show you how.

This one-of-a-kind book will help you to:

- ♦ Take authority over demonic spirits
- ♦ Conduct a private 2-hour prayer appointment
- ♦ Administer a 15-page diagnostic questionnaire
- ♦ Break bondages of rejection, addiction, lust, and more
- ♦ Bring inner healing and break soul ties
- ♦ Set free those whom the enemy has held captive

All this rooted in solid, biblical integrity and done in a calm, safe, controlled ministry environment.

Paperback (201 pp.) • 1.58502.002.8 • **$10.80 (save 10%)**

CONFRONTING THE QUEEN OF HEAVEN

C. Peter Wagner

This book takes a look at what is perhaps one of the most powerful spirits in Satan's hierarchy--the Queen of Heaven. This book answers what we as Christians can do to play a part in confronting the Queen of Heaven and proclaiming that Jesus Christ is Lord.

Paperback (42 pp.) • 0.9667481.3.1 • **$5.40 (save 10%)**

PRAYING THROUGH TURKEY
AN INTERCESSOR'S GUIDE TO AN ANCIENT AND NEEDY LAND

Andrew Jackson with George Otis, Jr.

This book will take you on a fantastic journey, tracing Christianity from its roots to modern times in the nation of Turkey. Intercessors will receive invaluable instruction on how to pray for the cities and unreached peoples of Turkey.

Paperback (60 pp.) • 1.58502.000.1 • **$5.40 (save 10%)**

Other titles available from Wagner Publications:

♦ SUPERNATURAL ARCHITECTURE
   by Dr. Stan DeKoven

♦ HOW TO HAVE A DYNAMIC CHURCH PRAYER MINISTRY, *by Jill Griffith*

For credit card orders please:
call *toll free* 1-888-563-5150
or fax 1-719-266-8256
or email: Arsenal@cpwagner.net

Or mail order with payment to:
The Arsenal
P.O. Box 62958
Colorado Springs, CO 80962-2958 USA

For bulk orders please:
call: 1-719-277-6776
or email: Wlsales@cpwagner.net

All international orders must be paid by credit card

Name _____

Street Address _____
(Cannot deliver to P.O. Box)

_____

Phone _____

Title	Product Number	Qty.	Total
	Subtotal (carry this amount to other side)		

Order form continued . . .

Shipping Rate Table for US only		Subtotal (from other side)	
Amt. of Subtotal	Add		
$50 and under	$5		
$50.01-$60.00	$6	CO residents add 6.01% sales tax	
$60.01-$80.00	$8		
$80.01-$100.00	$10		
Over $100.00	10% of order		
For international orders, please call or fax with credit card. Shipping will be calculated for you.		Shipping (see table)	
		Donation to GHM	
		TOTAL ENCLOSED (US FUNDS ONLY)	

Please allow 10 days for delivery. International orders may require 6 weeks for delivery.

METHOD OF PAYMENT:

☐ Check/Money Order (made payable to The Arsenal)

☐ Credit Card: ☐   ☐   ☐ 🔲 🔳

Number: _____

Exp. Date: _____ Signature: _____